An American citizen for 39 years, Ralph Fabri was born in Budapest, Hungary, where he studied architecture and creative arts at the Royal Institute of Technology and the Royal Academy of Fine Arts. He is a member and officer of many leading art organizations, including Britain's Royal Society of Arts, Audubon Artists (Honorary Life President), the Society of American Graphic Artists, and the American Watercolor Society. He was one of the art editors of Funk and Wagnall's UNIVERSAL STANDARD ENCYCLOPEDIA.

Mr. Fabri is currently Associate Professor at the City College of New York and Associate Editor of the magazine TODAY'S ART. He is the author of LEARN TO DRAW (1945), and OIL PAINTING, HOW TO-DO-IT (1953), a bestseller in its field. Ralph Fabri has exhibited in most national exhibitions as well as in Italy, France, England, India, Egypt, and elsewhere around the world. He has a long list of awards and honorable mentions. The author's works are in many permanent collections, including The Metropolitan Museum of Art, The National Academy, The New York Public Library, The Library of Congress, and the Smithsonian Institution.

THE ART OF POLYMER PAINTING

THE ART OF POLYMER PAINTING

By Ralph Fabri

 Reinhold Publishing Corporation/New York

COLOR ILLUSTRATIONS

© 1966 Reinhold Publishing Corporation
All rights reserved
Printed in the United States of America
Library of Congress Catalog Card Number: 66-22685

Designed by Emilio Squeglio
Printed by The Guinn Company, Inc.
Bound by A. Horowitz & Son
Color by Minerva Printing Corp.
Published by Reinhold Publishing Corporation
430 Park Avenue, New York, N.Y.

CONTENTS

Introduction

Prehistoric artists, whose pictures served the magic purposes of assuring power over beasts and pacifying the spirits of the dead, made their drawings on the walls of caves with charred sticks of wood. They noticed that fat dripping from roasting meat turned the earth into a soft, colored substance and used this for painting. Much later, the equally accidental discovery of glazes enabled man to manufacture more attractive as well as more durable bricks. The classical Greeks painted with encaustics, pigments bound by wax. Mixing pigments with eggwhite or the whole egg led to tempera painting. In medieval times, workers trying to decorate white plaster walls by painting them with pigments dissolved in water realized that such paint would become an integral part of the plaster as it dried. This was the beginning of the great art of fresco painting.

Oil painting, unquestionably practiced in ancient times, was forgotten during the Dark Ages until the brothers Hubert and Jan Van Eyck rediscovered and introduced it in Flanders at around the turn of the fifteenth century. Watercolor has also been known for a long time; it was the medium of illuminators of manuscripts. Medieval artists made sketches in pen-and-ink and washes, occasionally in color, although watercolor, as we understand it, was not introduced until the eighteenth century, when Paul Sandby and John Robert Cozens used it in England. In gouache, a related technique, the colors used are opaque, mixed with white. Shortly before World War II, casein was introduced, the first water-thinned paint to dry waterproof.

One can never truly pinpoint the beginning of any new idea, but it is believed that Mexican artists, in search of bright colors for outdoor use, were the first to experiment with plastic paint. Probably at the same time, American artists also tried to work with quick-drying, waterproof automobile enamels on Masonite and other boards. Now polymer, as a new medium, came upon the art scene with a real bang.

WHAT IS POLYMER?

Ours is an age of plastics. It was inevitable that plastics should also be employed in the fine arts. This book will not go into the chemistry of polymer emulsion paints. Suffice it to say that pigments are now mixed with synthetic, that is, man-made, plastic binders, produced by the chemical process called polymerization. Most synthetic artists' colors on the market today have binders made from chemicals of the acrylic and vinyl families. Some are based on acrylic resin alone; in others acrylic and vinyl are joined to form an acrylic-vinyl copolymer. For convenience, they can all be referred to as polymer paints.

This book deals with polymers that are suspended in water. Those that require thinners or solvents such as turpentine are briefly described in a special chapter on page 90.

7

WHY WORK IN POLYMER?

We expect everything new to be better than what we used to have, whether it is a refrigerator, a cereal or a detergent. As many highly advertised items have turned out to be no better than the old ones, we have become skeptical. "Is polymer superior to all the other painting media?" you might ask. The answer is that no painting medium is better than the others; each has properties which make it more practical or more inspiring under certain circumstances than others. You can make an outdoor sketch in watercolor, crayon, feltbrush, for example; why carry a big box of polymer? Every medium has drawbacks. Casein is practical for outdoor painting as it dries fast, but colors look lighter dry than when you apply them; and it is very difficult to obtain really dark tones with it. Oils are still wonderful for indoor painting, but they become muddy if you try to make changes in the wet paint. It is easy to lighten them by adding white but troublesome to make them darker and to paint fine details unless you wait days for the paint to dry.

Polymer eliminates these and other problems. The paint dries almost instantly, although you can manage to keep it wet for a while by adding water. You can change your picture immediately, any number of times, without muddying your colors. Paint the sky, for example, and, minutes later, do the lacelike branches and foliage of trees right over it. Casein has a powdery quality, nice for old, plastered buildings, but not so satisfactory when soft blending is desirable. Polymer blends as easily as oils do. The finest lines are possible in polymer by using a wet, pointed brush. Impasto is a "natural" in polymer, whereas in casein, it will crack and chip off within a short time. In oils, impasto takes a long time to build up; it is not going to retain its original shape and size.

Impasto is one extreme of polymer; the other extreme is to employ it like transparent aquarelle. You can flood the paper with a cloudburst, but this dries in minutes, waterproof, so that you can go into it with any other color, wet or dry, thick or thin; paint bright yellow over bright·blue, red over black and so forth.

There are purists, of course, who say that real aquarelle must be done with watercolor and real oil paintings must be done in oils. The purists are wrong. In art, it is the final result that counts. Polymer offers sensational freedom for self-expression in any style. You can work all day long; with brushes, knives, trowels; you can build your paint up, cut it like wood; paint on any surface, except an oily one. Polymer paintings can be varnished immediately, not a year-and-a-half later, as with oils; they need no glass for protection. When varnished, they become practically scuffproof. You can also add any object to polymer as it is a powerful adhesive. The greatest advantage of polymer is its versatility or, if we are permitted to coin a word: its experimentability. No other medium gives you the wide latitude in styles, techniques, textures, and the choice of surface on which to work as polymer does. Try it for yourself.

1. Materials for Polymer Painting

Polymer adheres to any surface except an oily one. Make a habit of reading the labels on all polymer materials. Remember the warning on TV commercials: "Use only as directed!"

Heavy-weight paper, illustration and multimedia boards are available at art supply stores; lumberyards sell Masonite. Any raw canvas or textile can be prepared for polymer by giving it a coat or two of polymer gesso. Such canvas may be rolled up when painted; it remains flexible, will not crack or chip off.

COLORS

All major manufacturers offer color charts free of charge. Each of them lists about thirty colors, more than you normally need, but you ought to have the following set, the names sometimes vary among manufacturers, for satisfactory results:

Cadmium red medium	Ultramarine blue
Alizarin crimson	Cobalt blue
Cadmium orange	Phthalocyanine blue
Cadmium yellow light	Phthalocyanine green
Cadmium yellow medium	Chromium oxide green
Yellow ochre	Ivory black
Burnt sienna	Cobalt violet

Titanium white (large tube)

Additional colors may be purchased if larger quantities of paint are needed, as for painting a mural or theatrical backdrop. Raw sienna, Hooker's green, Payne's gray, manganese blue are valuable supplements.

Polymer can be purchased either in jars or tubes. The jar colors are usually not as thick as tube colors. Used as they come from the jar, they give the effect of opaque watercolor, gouache or tempera. Thinned with water, they resemble transparent watercolor. If they are not as thick as oil colors, they will soon thicken to oil consistency on your palette. The tube colors have a body similar to oils as they come from the tube and are thinned with water when used as watercolor or tempera.

Paint can be taken from jars with wooden spoons or tongue depressors; open jars can be covered with a sheet of household aluminum foil until you are finished with the day's work. If a skin forms on any paint, remove it.

BRUSHES

For watercolor technique, use regular watercolor brushes: flat and round sables. Otherwise, work with flat bristle brushes and a couple of flat and round sables for finishing touches and finer details. Buy good-quality brushes. It is most annoying to be compelled to pick hairs out of your paint all the time.

A long-bladed palette knife and a small, trowel-shaped painting knife are good to have, for scraping the palette and for applying impasto.

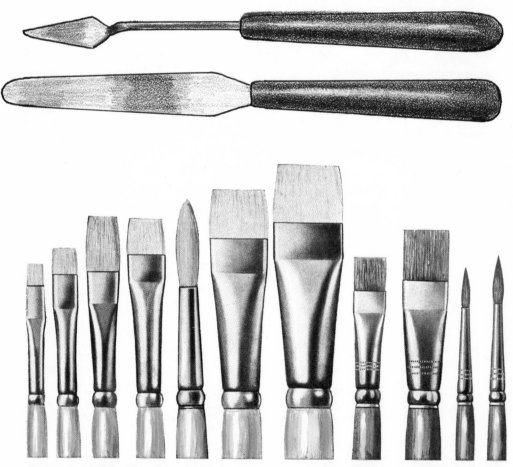

Recommended brushes (left to right): quarter-inch "bright", three-eighths "bright", half-inch "flat", nine-sixteenths "bright", quarter-inch "round", three-quarter-inch and one-inch "brights", all bristle brushes; half-inch and five-eighths flat sables, two small round sables. "Brights" are thin, flat brushes, "flats" are thicker, with longer bristles, "rounds" are round. Painting knife (top), and palette knife are useful for painting and scraping.

10

YOUR PALETTE AND HOW TO USE IT

Wood or enameled metal palettes are not recommended for polymer. Use paper palettes or new plastic palettes designed for polymer, equipped with special covers. A glass palette is fine if you have a safe place for it. Polymer can be scraped off the glass with the palette knife.

Establish a system for laying your colors on the palette, instead of placing them any old way. A good system is to have white in the center, the warm colors (yellow, orange, red, brown) on one side, and the cool colors (greens and blues) on the other. Black may be at either end. Place them about an inch from the top and an inch from each other for best results. Leave the rest of the palette for mixing.

Before you start painting, place at least a little of each color on the palette. Do not think that because you are about to paint a red apple, all you need is red paint. That apple has red, orange, yellow, brown, black, blue, white, ochre in it. As polymer dries fast, put only as much paint on the palette as you expect to use up within a short time.

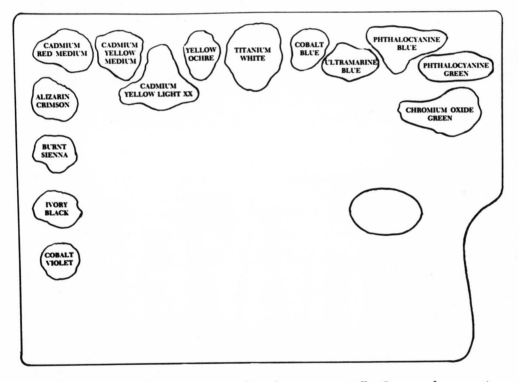

Palette: acquire the habit of arranging the colors systematically. Leave a large section for mixing.

MODELING PASTE AND EXTENDER

A remarkable substance, prepared with white marble dust, modeling paste is a most stimulating feature of polymer painting. It dries quickly and retains its shape. It can be mixed with any color as a thickening agent. I prefer to apply it as it comes from the can, build it up with knife, brush, spoon to the desired thickness and texture, allow it to dry, then paint it. You can create a true relief with the extender. Some artists believe that a painting ought to be nothing but a painting; I do not agree with this notion. Textural effects enhance the beauty of a painting, especially when the picture is varnished and the glossy surface catches the light.

GEL

This gelatinous, vaseline-like material comes in tubes and may be mixed with any color in order to give the paint bulk and make it transparent without reducing its original brilliance or strength. I have discovered that if I apply gel without mixing it with any color, it absorbs the color over which it is used so that I need not paint it if that color happens to be what I want. Try both the extender and gel, separately, or the transparent gel over opaque extender textures. It is fascinating to experiment with new materials. It leads to new ideas.

MEDIA

Polymer can be thinned with as much or as little water as you like. There are also two kinds of media, matte and glossy, both of which serve for varnishing the finished painting as well as for controlling the degree of gloss. A few drops of the medium in the water in which you rinse your brushes or on each color on the palette will give your painting a uniform sheen or high gloss, depending upon which medium you employ. I prefer to work without a medium, but varnish my paintings as soon as they are finished. Either medium may be used in glazing but, actually, all you need is plain water for thinning down any color.

OTHER SUPPLIES

If you drop or spill polymer on clothes, floor, furniture, wash it off immediately with water. Polymer solvents do exist, but they are flammable and poisonous. Wash brushes after use in soap and lukewarm water. Household cleaning liquids, such as Mr. Clean, seem to help. If you forget to wash a brush and it dries hard, soak it in denatured alcohol for a while.

Have at least two cans of water on hand and wear a smock or apron while working with polymer. Paint on a table, a slanted drawing board or on an easel, depending upon your style. If you work like an aquarellist, with lots of water, a flat position is necessary. Working on an easel permits you to step back, every now and then, to look at your painting from a distance.

2. Main Techniques in Polymer Painting

AQUARELLE TECHNIQUE

Polymer is one of the so-called *aquamedia*, paint used with water. If you are a watercolorist, you will probably start to work with polymer as if it were aquarelle. You can achieve the same transparent, airy effects that have made watercolor so popular. Use the same kind of paper and brushes, plenty of water. The result will be exactly like a true watercolor . . . why, then, use polymer?

Because polymer dries almost instantly and one color covers any other color. Corrections, changes are easy, without scrubbing or scraping. In regular watercolor, you must leave the paper unpainted for white clouds or for delicate pastel shades; only dark colors have a chance of covering light ones. In polymer, you can paint white clouds on top of a blue sky, apply the palest yellow over black or red. In other words, polymer makes watercolor painting easy.

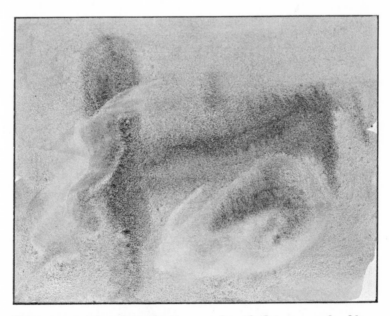

Transparent aquarelle technique: work with flat or round sable brushes as in regular watercolor. Polymer colors cover each other.

OIL PAINTING TECHNIQUE

Work on any non-oily surface. Add a little water at first but, most of the time, use polymer as it comes from jar or tube. You have to work fast as the paint dries quickly. The result, especially if the painting is varnished, is just like a real oil painting . . . why, then, use polymer?

Oil painting technique: use flat bristle brushes. Apply paint in various directions to achieve an appearance of smoothness.

Because fast-drying polymer allows you to paint one color on any other color without muddying your work or waiting days for the paint to dry. Furthermore, no matter how thick the polymer may be, it remains absolutely flexible. You can roll it up and unroll it anytime. In a way, polymer makes oil painting easy.

Parallel brush strokes create the effect of a downpour, alternating horizontal and vertical strokes, that of a basket or floormat.

POLYMER TECHNIQUE

Polymer is not meant to and never will eliminate oils, tempera, aquarelle, casein and other established media. It is something new; and it offers new possibilities, new excitement. The logical approach is to explore and utilize it as fully as possible, to create paintings that you could not execute in another medium.

Certain techniques are bound to evolve naturally from the characteristics of the new material. For instance, start with thin washes to establish the general color effect. Then work with little, if any, water, building up the biggest forms, masses and tones. Go over these with any number of transparent washes; they lend your painting a glow, a depth, impossible to achieve in any other manner. The Old Masters used glazing in their oil paintings, often over tempera underpaintings. Polymer glazes demonstrate the versatility of the medium. They can be easily interrupted by thicker applications of paint, even heavy impasto. One glaze may be spread over another without any delay, as if you were placing transparencies of different colors over an electric light. Exploit the potentialities of polymer and, at the end, your work will look what it really is: an effective polymer painting.

Polymer technique: start with washes; follow with thicker paint, using little or no water; add impasto; finish with glazes to pull the painting together.

16

IMPASTO TECHNIQUE

Impasto refers to a thick application of paint, possible heretofore only in oils. Rembrandt used impasto in some of his paintings, like "Man in a Gold Helmet," in which the helmet decorations are quite thick. When doing an impasto, consider the following points:

1) Work on gessoed Masonite, plywood or heavy multimedia board, rather than on paper or light canvas.

2) Do not apply paint in big heaps. Build the work up gradually, giving a little time between layers for the paint to dry inside.

3) For extra-heavy impasto, use the extender; let it dry hard before painting over it.

4) The purpose of impasto ought to be esthetic; it must be an integral part of the picture. In a representational painting, the impasto should be based on reality. For example, in a tree trunk, apply the paint in strokes indicating the bark of the tree; in water, make the impasto look like ripples or waves; in rocks, try to simulate cracks and crevices. See the color illustration, "Moraine Lake near Banff," on page 55, in which I have used impasto in such a manner as to indicate textures.

The addition of a few drops of medium in the impasto is helpful, but not necessary.

Impasto: apply large forms with palette knife, smaller ones with trowel-shaped painting knife, indicating texture with the strokes. Do the work gradually rather than in big heaps.

COLLAGE

Collage is a French word which rhymes with *garage* and means a paste-up. The French word sounds more impressive. Collage may be representational or abstract. Most collages are combined with painted parts. One may have reservations about collage. Why glue paper, textiles, and so forth on canvas or board instead of painting the entire subject? Such questions are academic. Contemporary artists are not required to produce photographic representations. Collage can be interesting and a lot of fun to do, but here, too, certain rules ought to be observed.

1) Work only with permanent materials.

2) There must be an esthetic composition, a pleasing color arrangement, or textural interest.

3) Consider the problem of keeping a collage safe and clean, You may cover it with plastic or frame it in a shadowbox covered with glass. Varnishing may suffice in some cases.

The most natural type of collage is a scene in which some actual objects are pasted on the picture. For instance, a seashore subject is painted realistically, with real pebbles, seashells, and even sand stuck right into the polymer paint.

In my collage "Big City," shown in color on page 55, I first painted the sky and the silhouettes of the buildings in a violet tone, the water in green and blue strokes, and indicated the rocks. I tore pieces of good-quality corrugated paper, cut strips of awnings, various colored paper and fabrics into the right shapes and sizes, pasting some of these over the silhouettes of houses and others on the water, with a lot of polymer or with a good white glue. The rocks are made of heavy tarpaper with some real rock on top and real pebbles, from an old aquarium, on the near-shore. Where I accidentally smudged the sky, I covered it up with a disk cut out of yellow paper, creating the effect of the sun.

The collage received a heavy coat of glossy varnish. When illuminated from one side, it looks especially striking.

Collage: paint the main forms in the simplest manner; tear or cut materials to the desired shapes and sizes; paste them on with plenty of polymer or with fast-drying glue.

3. Basic Features of Representational Painting

SKETCHING

Present-day art may be divided into two main categories: representational and nonrepresentational, or nonobjective. We will define the term "representational" as any painting, sculpture or graphic art whose subject is recognizable, even if far from photographic realism. This book deals with representational art, not as if this were the only true art, as many persons contend, but because the best-known "modern" artists started out with representational work and developed their own, often strange or bizarre, styles afterward. Representational art begins with sketching, from actual observation or from imagination.

Sketching develops skill. It keeps you from wasting time on endless changes while working on a final painting. The better your sketch, the more familiar you are with your subject, the more sparkle you can put into your finished work.

I make small sketches, often one on top of the other, until I feel I have my idea worked out fairly well. I outline the last sketch in red ink or crayon and redraw it on a clean sheet of paper, in the same proportions as my painting is to be. If the subject is simple, I draw it directly on my board. If it is complicated, I prefer to square it up, the way artists do when they plan a mural.

To do this, draw horizontal and vertical lines in pencil over the sketch, half-an-inch or an inch apart, according to the complexity of the subject. Draw the same number of horizontal and vertical lines on the board or canvas, on a correspondingly larger scale, in charcoal. Copy the original, one square after another. Then go over the drawing lines with a small brush dipped in a neutral color, such as yellow ochre, wipe the charcoal off, and you have completed a neat layout for the painting.

Another method is to cover the board with a sheet of tracing paper fastened with Scotch masking tape and to draw the layout on it in charcoal. Go over the final outlines in pencil and wipe the charcoal off. Trace the outlines on the board with the help of a carbon paper. Do not use a typewriter carbon, but prepare one yourself by coating a sheet of thin paper with graphite or an ordinary soft pencil. Slip this sheet under the tracing paper, face down. The dye in the typewriter carbon might smudge your colors. Your own carbon paper may be saved and used many times.

Sketch of Cambodian dancers. I often draw one sketch on top of the other, outlining the last one in red ink or crayon.

I redraw a complicated subject and divide it into squares.

then **draw** the same number of squares on the final board and enlarge the sketch by copying it square-by-square. Small details are not necessary.

COMPOSITION

By dictionary definition, composition is the art or practice of so combining the parts of a work of art as to produce a harmonious whole. To the artist, composition is the design which holds the work of art together in such a manner that we cannot remove any part of it without destroying the esthetic appearance of the entire work. This does not imply that there can only be one good composition for a given subject.

Styles, tastes, techniques have changed during the twenty-six centuries of Western Civilization. The ancient Greeks and, after them, the Romans, liked symmetry in their art, and this concept predominated in Renaissance art as well. The Baroque Period of the seventeenth and eighteenth centuries, however, was dedicated to asymmetrical, often turbulent, composition and off-centered design prevails in contemporary art. One universal feature of artistic composition is *not* to depict objects as if they were displayed in a store on a shelf. They must be combined into plausible and pleasing or interesting groups.

Certain psychological factors are also involved. An object painted close to the bottom appears to be very small and sinking or falling out of the picture. Painted close to the top, the object may seem to be flying. Placed in the center, with much space left all round, an object looks very small, while painting the same object as tall as the entire canvas causes it to look gigantic, regardless of the actual size of the picture. If it is too close to one edge of the painting and looks or points inward, it creates the feeling that someone or something is just entering the scene; if it is close to the edge and looks or points outward, the impression is that it is leaving the picture for good. If the subject, whatever it may be, spreads over the entire picture it is more like an over-all design, perhaps for a wallpaper, than a work of fine art.

Although there is no law against symmetry, avoid placing a tall object in the exact center, with smaller items right and left, or painting tall objects close to the left and right edges, with a small item in the center. Avoid painting vertical forms, such as trees, too close to the upright edges of your picture or painting horizontal forms, such as logs or a road, too close to the bottom. Such objects make the frame appear wider and the picture smaller.

Renaissance artists followed the Graeco-Roman tradition of symmetry. The main figure is always in the center; right and left are balanced.

Artists of the Baroque period were more restless; they preferred asymmetry. The main figure is always off center.

We still favor the asymmetrical layout. This is the basic composition of a landscape by André Dunoyer de Segonzac (1930).

A completely symmetrical landscape looks stiff.

The same elements here are too far on one side.

This off-centered arrangement is most natural.

Psychology of composition: object here is too small, precisely centered, so low that it appears to be sinking.

Same object now seems to be traveling along a trolley wire. The horizontal table divides the picture into what could be stripes of a flag.

Object is large enough, but seems to be sliding downhill.

Object filling the b[ox] gives the effect o[f] wallpaper design.

Person appears to be just walking in, and will no matter what you put in the background: room or scenery.

Person is walking out, turning his back on the world.

The pitcher and the fruits seem to be accidentally rolling in.

The same items are [?] exiting, like a duck [and] her ducklings.

PERSPECTIVE

Perspective is the visual appearance of objects and scenes. It is also the art or science of depicting three-dimensional forms on a two-dimensional surface. With the sole exception of the sphere, all objects look different from every viewpoint. We use both line and color to create perspective. Drawing humans and animals in perspective is called foreshortening.

LINEAR PERSPECTIVE

The ancient Greeks, with their keen perceptions and analytical minds, discovered the rules of receding lines. They were the first to depict foreshortening quite correctly, to show human hands and feet as they look from all angles. Perspective is literally a science as well as an art. Its laws can be calculated geometrically, but they can also be seen with the naked eye, providing the eye is trained to see everything on a flat plane, rather than in space, eliminating the so-called memory pictures of ancient civilizations.

In Egyptian painting, the face was shown in profile, eye and shoulders were depicted from the front, the rest of the body and legs from the side; hands in certain positions were reversed; a person usually had two right feet or two left feet. An Egyptian artist would represent a batch of pottery on a horizontal line, all urns of the same size, just overlapping each other.

An untrained person draws objects the same way in our own century, with a row of houses on a street all seen directly from the front, their doors and windows rectangular; cars seen from the side. His book "looks like a book" to him only when he draws it as an oblong, the shape in which the book is actually printed and bound. Perspective is easy to understand when reduced to a few basic concepts.

Cut a square piece of cardboard; draw a circle on it, touching the center point of each side of the square. Then draw vertical, horizontal and two diagonal lines across the center. Observe this from various angles: from every viewpoint, the square, the circle, and the lines themselves change in form or direction and size. The same changes occur in the visual appearance of all shapes, except the sphere, as noted before.

In a street scene, the changes may seem bigger, but the principle is the same. The other end of a book looks only a little narrower than the near end, while the far end of a city block looks much smaller than the end near you. It can all be boiled down to a few principles:

1) Objects appear to diminish the farther away they are.

2) Vertical lines remain vertical in perspective, but horizontal lines seem to converge in the distance. Lines above your eye level seem to be going downward, lines below your eye level go upward.

3) Parallel horizontal lines appear to run together into one point, the so-called "vanishing point" on the horizon, which is your eye level. The eye level is not a fixed line; it goes up and down with you. The horizon is clearly seen on the sea: the line where the water meets the sky. In hilly scenery or in a crowded city, you cannot see the horizon, but it is the level of your own eyes. In a row of houses, all horizontal lines, windowsills, eaves and so forth, converge into the same vanishing point. If you see two sides of a corner building the parallel lines on one side run into one vanishing point, the parallel lines on the other side run into another, but both of them are on the same horizon or eye level. Houses, lampposts, telegraph poles, cars, persons look smaller and smaller in the distance.

An architectural renderer can draw a perfect image of a building from the architect's plans, there is no reason why an artist or art student should not be able to draw a view from actual observation. One thing to watch, is not to exaggerate the perspective.

The ancient Egyptians had a naïve idea of perspective; proportions meant little to them. Tradition decreed how figures and objects should be represented. Note that the man has two left hands and two left feet. The right hand of each woman is not really holding the stem of the lotus flower; their left hands are actually the right hands. These are so-called "memory pictures."

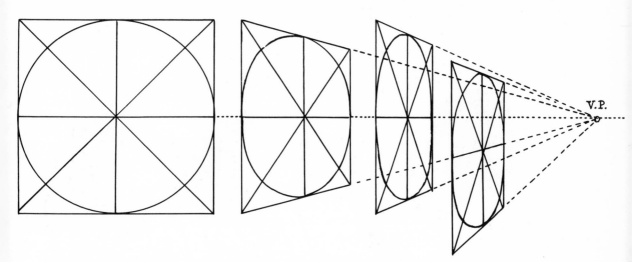

V.P.

Try this demonstration for yourself, following the directions given on page 25. As you turn the cardboard, its own form as well as the circle, and all lines look different from every angle.

The same changes occur in any object, except the sphere. A book is here seen standing up, slanting, and flat on the table.

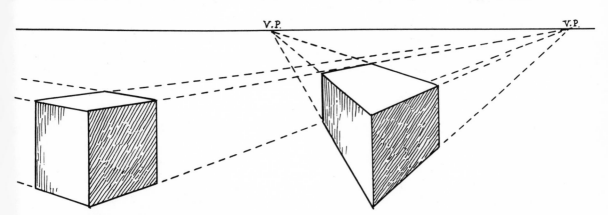

V.P.   V.P.

At least one of the vanishing points should be quite far to the right or left; otherwise, the perspective becomes exaggerated.

To a beginner in art, a street is always seen from the front; every window and door is a fully visible rectangle.

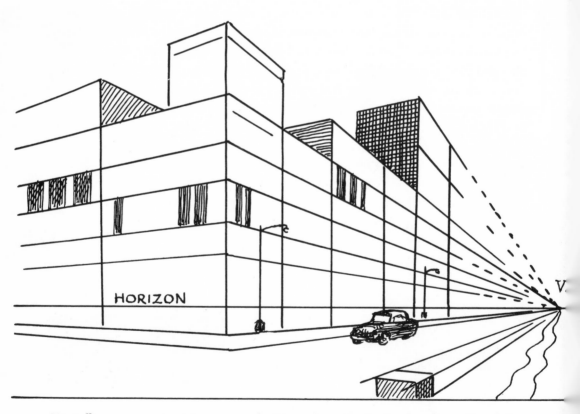

HORIZON

V.

Normally, we see a street from an angle. Lines above the horizon go down, lines below the horizon go up. All parallel lines run into a vanishing point (V. P.) on the horizon.

COLOR PERSPECTIVE AND VALUES

Not until the Early Renaissance did artists notice that faraway hills and objects are bluish in tone. They still depicted the tiniest details, though. It was the great achievement of the Impressionists of about a hundred years ago to discover the vital importance of color in painting. They discovered that distance, weather, the time of day affect the strength of every color. The morning sun radiates a yellowish tone; the afternoon sun is warmer in color; the evening sun throws a reddish veil over the entire scenery; on a cloudy day, everything is grayish. Houses are often a bright violet against the brilliant sunset which turns windows into blinding orange lights.

It is of the utmost significance to realize that colors vary in intensity, that the lightest color we have is white, the darkest black, and all other colors must be between these two extremes. "Value" refers to the strength of any hue when compared with white and black, how much darker it is than the one and how much lighter than the other. Red, green, blue, brown, violet, and so on are different hues, but a very pale blue may be no darker than a strong yellow. In other words, the two totally different hues may have exactly the same value.

If you give a color too dark a value, it will look like a hole in your picture; if you give it too light a value it will appear to be a piece of paper stuck onto your painting. The Old Masters used to include some white material in their paintings so they could more ably compare the values of colors. You might, at least temporarily, place a piece of white paper or a handkerchief near the lightest item in your subject. You are bound to notice how much darker the item is than white.

Color perspective requires comparing every color with white and black. All shades of every hue are somewhere between these two extremes. The closer a color is to white, the higher its value.

LIGHT AND SHADOW

With perhaps the sole exception of the Romans, ancient artists used no light and shadow in their paintings; oriental artists knew nothing about light and shadow until recent times. Yet, without light and shadow, truly realistic pictures are impossible. What makes the paintings of Renaissance and Baroque artists absolutely three-dimensional is the full comprehension of light and shadow as well as linear and color perspective.

By daylight, the edges of shadows are much softer than by artificial light. Observe lights and shadows as you would any other part of your subject; each light and shadow has a shape, a size, a color and a value of its own. The highlight is the brightest part. On a sphere, it is the spot closest to the source of light; on a cone, it is a straight line from tip to bottom. On round objects, the shadow is darkest slightly inside the edge; the edge itself has a reflected light which is always less bright than the illuminated side of the round object.

Cast shadow is the shadow thrown by one object on another. The shape of this shadow is a combination of the form of the object itself and the shape and position of the surface on which it is cast. The color of any shadow depends upon illumination and the actual, so-called local color of each object. Do not take any shape or color for granted. Observe everything. Study the works of Old Masters and present-day magic realists. Although not many artists are now interested in perfect realism, representational art demands at least an understanding of the problems involved. You may create an interesting picture without a single shadow, just as the Chinese and Japanese did for many centuries, but if you do paint shadows. paint them correctly.

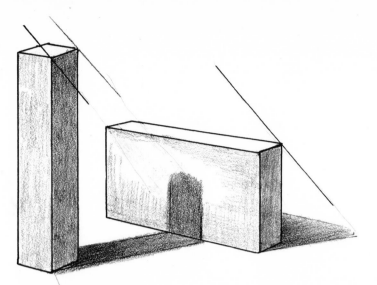

Light and shadow: the part of an object closest to the source of light is brightest; the farthest part is darkest. Every illuminated article casts a shadow, stronger in artificial than natural light. This shadow follows the form upon which it falls.

On round forms, the darkest area is found a little inside the edge; the edge holds a reflected light which is not as bright as the illuminated part.

The same facts apply to natural objects, such as a pear and an apple.

4. Color Mixing

In physics, red, yellow and blue are the so-called primary colors from which all other colors can be mixed. In art, however, we need at least two different hues of each of the primaries, besides white and black, although some artists prefer to work without black. With the exception of aquarelle, white is mixed with practically every color and you have to buy it in a bigger tube than any other.

The color-mixing chart in this book is somewhat different from the usual ones. It is divided into eight horizontal stripes and twelve vertical columns, as you can see in the color illustration on page 42.

The importance of having two considerably different hues of each primary is best proved by the mixtures you can obtain. For example, alizarin crimson and white give you pink, while cadmium red medium and white mix into peach. A little black turns yellow into a greenish color. You can avoid using black and still obtain very dark colors by mixing ultramarine blue with violet or phthalocyanine green, or alizarin crimson with the same green.

Each mixture is naturally influenced by the proportions of the ingredients. For a bluish green, increase the amount of blue, for a reddish orange, increase the amount of red, and so forth. Adding white makes any color lighter, but it also may create a "chalky" effect. It is often better to lighten a hue by mixing it with a lighter color of the same group. Add orange and/or yellow to red; add yellow to green. Experiment with various mixtures. You can add a little alizarin crimson to cobalt blue to make the blue "warmer"; burnt sienna or cadmium red makes green softer, warmer; white and perhaps a dash of blue will turn a color "cooler." Even black can be made warmer or cooler by adding a touch of red or blue. As a matter of fact, practically all colors should be mixed rather than used as they come from jar or tube. Pure colors are best for poster designs.

A good example of the immense number of colors we find around us is demonstrated in my painting, "Quiet Street in Taormina," shown in color on page 43. Since ancient times, Taormina has been considered one of the beauty spots of the world. It rises high above the Gulf of Catania in Sicily. Hundreds of houses painted in pastel shades sparkle in the sunlight as they climb higher and higher. Along narrow, winding roads tall, slender cypress trees lead to the summit, a Graeco-Roman amphitheater from which you see a superb panorama.

Every house has been painted many times, in various colors or shades. The plaster crumbles or peels off; patches of previous coats of paint show through among newer ones. Not only every house, but almost every floor is a different shade. Doors, their jambs, window frames and shutters also vary in color. This, truly, is a paradise for those who love color.

I made sketches, took snapshots and notes. My painting is not a photographic replica of the actual street, but it is in the exact spirit of the ancient town, with its mixture of shabby and new or at least newly repaired and painted houses, quiet on a cloudy afternoon when most of the people were at work or in the bustling tourist center of Taormina. I tried to capture the mother-of-pearl tones of this deserted part of a famous and certainly not poverty-stricken Sicilian town.

The color illustration includes a chart of colors I used in the mixtures needed for this rich-hued scene.

5. Color Effects

Every color should be considered in relationship to the ones around it. Yellow, for instance, looks much brighter when surrounded by blue than when its neighbors are white, light pink or peach. Even size is affected by color combination. A black square on a white background appears smaller than a white square of the same size on a black background. Certain colors seem to jump out, others to recede, according to the hues around them, as you might notice by looking at the color-mixing chart on page 42.

One problem in painting is to render glowing objects, such as lamps, neon signs. Phosphorescent, luminous paints exist for commercial purposes only. They quickly lose their brilliance and turn quite dark; no self-respecting artists should employ them in a work of art. You have to achieve the effect of illumination with the help of color relationships. Contrasts are helpful, but not sufficient. A few hints follow:

Yellow is brighter with a pale blue outline which gradually blends into light green, blue-green, and darker green. A very light green outline blending into blue and violet causes an orange-colored object to seem brighter. Try various combinations until you obtain the right result.

Some optical effects are illustrated in color on page 54. There are three colored rows on the top of the board, one black, one white, one cobalt blue with four squares in each row. From left to right, yellow; orange; green; peach. Each of the squares in the top row contains a small cobalt blue square. In the second row, the small squares are red. In the third row, they are pale blue. Yellow and peach look much lighter on black than on white; blue and red appear much darker on yellow and peach than on orange and green; the pale blue seems to be much lighter on orange and green than on yellow and peach.

Below the squares, observe how the effect of glowing is created. In the upper left, a candle flame is rendered realistically. It is not just a yellow tongue, but a blue core turning into violet, pale yellow, medium yellow with an orange tip, greenish outline, and purple tone around the flame.

The rectangular and elliptical shapes glow because they are surrounded by shades of other hues, blending gradually into the dark background. The brightness of the column of six round spots is influenced by the green, blue and violet background colors.

The flames in the lower right have pale blue, green and violet tones as well as orange streaks. Without these, the fire would look like a piece of yellow paper cut in the shape of flames and pasted on a sheet of black paper.

It is impossible to list all the possibilities. My advice is, once again: Experiment on your own.

6. Still Life Painting

Still life provides inexhaustible material for painters. Art students seem to believe it is a subject for beginners or amateurs. That's as if a singer thought a Schubert song should be sung only by beginners, and that an accomplished singer should always sing operatic arias. Although we can see many still lifes in ancient Pompeii, the subject was not introduced as an important branch of Western art until the seventeenth century, when puritanic Protestants objected to Biblical, mythological and historical themes as idolatrous. Many "modern" artists have painted and are producing still lifes, often in combination with figures.

You can set up a still life anywhere, anytime, especially if you construct a shadowbox of plywood or, even more simply, just tear off the top and two sides of a large corrugated box from your supermarket to make a setting. You can then store your still life in the box, ready to work on whenever you have the time. Fresh fruits, vegetables, flowers do not keep, but they can easily be replaced with similar fresh ones. Other objects do not change or deteriorate. Nowadays, artificial flowers and fruits are so lifelike that you cannot tell what is real and what is plastic from a short distance. Books, silver and glassware, boxes, household objects, gloves, hats; rocks, driftwood, seashells, bric-à-brac are available in any house. Small statues, stuffed animals are not difficult to find.

Some people say that every still life subject has already been painted. For that matter, so have figures and nudes in every position, Biblical themes, scenery, trees, rivers, mountains, farmhouses! Originality in the arrangement is always possible; style and technique are bound to be the artist's own. Ultimately, what matters is not the subject, but how you present it and how much enjoyment you find in painting it.

How to Paint a Still Life:

STEP-BY-STEP DEMONSTRATION

For my demonstration, I selected a gaily-colored, Italian ceramic bowl, a banana, a red apple, a green pear, a Bosc pear, a bottle of Chianti, a stemmed glass with wine, and an open book, arranged on a pink tablecloth. The combination is quite natural; one might sit at a table reading a book while sampling a piece of fruit and a sip of wine. There is nothing strikingly original about it, but it is a challenge to paint the diverse textures, colors, and shapes. Note that the table is not seen horizontally, but from an angle to make it more interesting. The simple background will not detract from the still life. I prefer to work on a heavy, rough multimedia board with a white gesso finish, but another artist might work on Masonite or a non-oily canvas. The technique is the same.

Step 1. After several attempts, I found a satisfactory composition for my "Still Life on Table" and drew the final layout on the board in charcoal, working in light, sketchy lines, without worrying about small details. Instead of fixing the charcoal lines with a spray, I dip a small bristle brush in water and yellow ochre, go over the charcoal lines, then wipe the charcoal off with a rag. The result is a drawing without any charcoal dust to get into the paint.

To see the painting in color in its stages of development, refer to page 46.

Step 2. Apply colors as directly as possible, with enough water for the brush to glide easily on the rough surface. Paint the colors you actually see. A red apple is not a red disk on which you later indicate shadow and highlight. Try to paint the darks and lights as they are. If there is an ochre spot on the apple, paint it immediately. The Bosc pear is a mixture of burnt si-

···jects gathered for my still life: a ceramic bowl, a banana, an Anjou pear, a Bosc pear, a red apple, a ···ss of wine, a bottle of Chianti, an open book, a pink tablecloth.

Four trial arrangements of the objects are not successful. They look artificial, crowded or stiff.

Final drawing for my "Still Life on Table"

enna, orange, yellow, and a little black. The banana is not all the same yellow; it has a greenish-brown shadow, green stem. Paint a little here, a little there, working all over the board, rather than trying to complete any particular section. Do a few strokes on the tablecloth and the background close to the objects.

When mixing colors, dip your brush into the one closest to the color you need, then add others until you obtain the correct shade. If the result does not look right, start over. As polymer dries almost immediately, changes are easy.

Step 3. Observe values, the intensity of each color as compared with white and black. Step back, every now and then; look squint-eyed at your work in order to evaluate better the general effect of light and dark masses. Avoid making objects larger than life-size.

The precision of details depends upon your temperament as well as your skill. Photographic reality is not expected nowadays. Avoid a monotonous texture by making brush strokes in many different directions, rather than working in parallel strokes.

Do not paint the background by going neatly around each object; such hard outlining usually creates the effect we call "ghosts." Work away from the contour of each item or toward it. A soft edge is preferable to a hard one. Do not leave unpainted spots.

Step 4. The final touches include highlights, a better definition of details, a few dark spots, such as what you see between some strands of straw on the bottle. Bristle brushes are likely to leave fuzzy edges where that is not desirable. Correct these with a round or flat sable brush or a sharp bristle brush.

The background should not be one solid color all over. You are not rendering an actual wall but painting the appearance of a wall or backdrop. The colors vary in appearance in different sections of the painting. The tablecloth, too, has a diversity of tones. Cast shadows on apple, pear, tablecloth are not black, and their edges blend softly into the other colors. Glass is transparent, but it causes distortions. The red wine is not just red paint; observe its translucent quality. The glass sparkles, but has no hard outlines.

Stop work when you believe a painting is finished. Put it aside for a couple of days, then look at it with fresh eyes. You might discover a mistake or two. One mistake found by yourself is worth twenty-five pointed out by another person. Maybe Confucius did not say this, but it is valid, just the same.

OTHER STILL LIFE SUBJECTS

The kind of still life you can assemble anytime: vase, flowers, bowl of fruit.

Studio table, books, art materials offer colorful possibilities.

Guatemalan native figures. I placed an apple in front of them to indicate the scale of the group.

Bottles of different shapes with colorful labels can be arranged in countless ways.

Color Mixing. See next page for color illustration.

1. The original colors
2. Each color mixed with alizarin crimson
3. Each color mixed with cadmium red medium
4. Each color mixed with cadmium yellow light
5. Each color mixed with cadmium yellow medium
6. Each color mixed with cobalt blue
7. Each color mixed with ultramarine blue
8. Each color mixed with phthalocyanine green
9. Each color mixed with cobalt violet
10. Each color mixed with white, less in upper square than in lower
11. Each color mixed with black
12. The original colors

A. Alizarin crimson
B. Cadmium red medium
C. Cadmium yellow light
D. Cadmium yellow medium
E. Cobalt blue
F. Ultramarine blue
G. Phthalocyanine green
H. Cobalt violet

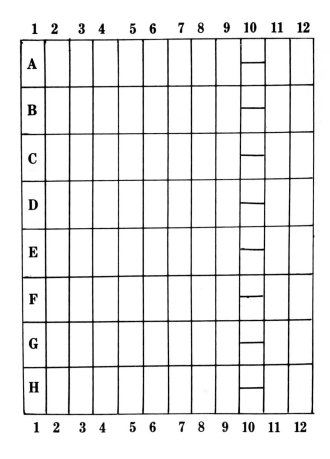

COLOR MIXING

See preceding page for list of colors and page 32 for description.

"QUIET STREET IN TAORMINA"

See following page for description of colors and color mixtures used in this painting.

Colors and mixtures used in "Quiet Street in Taormina". See color illustration on preceding page.

1. A very little phthalocyanine blue in white for the sky.
2. Shadow in clouds made with ivory black and alizarin crimson.
3. White, black, with alizarin and phthalocyanine green washes.
4. Black, white, burnt sienna.
5. Same, with an orange wash.
6. Ultramarine blue, white, with phthalocyanine green and black washes.
7. Burnt sienna, alizarin, cobalt blue.
8. Orange, yellow ochre, with alizarin and black washes.
9. Violet, white, cadmium red medium.
10. Burnt sienna, cadmium red.
11. Violet, phthalocyanine green with ultramarine blue wash.
12. Yellow ochre, violet, burnt sienna with black wash.
13. Yellow ochre, cobalt blue, white.
14. Ultramarine blue, white.
15. Chromium oxide green, cobalt blue, alizarin.
16. Same, but darker, with black wash.
17. Yellow ochre, black, alizarin.
18. Same with burnt sienna.
19. Roof: cadmium red, burnt sienna, black, orange.
20. Door and window shade: chromium oxide green, yellow ochre, black.
21. Burnt sienna, chromium oxide green, black.
22. Black, cobalt blue, yellow ochre, white.
23. Open doors, windows: ultramarine blue or chromium oxide green, with cadmium red.
24. Orange, yellow ochre, with black wash.
25. Shadows obtained by going over basic colors with one or more washes of alizarin, violet and black.

"Old Hotel, Bushkill, Pa." a picturesque wooden structure with ill-assorted additions.

STEP 2.

STEP 3.

"STILL LIFE ON TABLE"

Work all over the board, and try to apply the right colors at once, instead of painting some basic hues, then going over those. Concentrate on important masses rather than on small details.

STEP 2.

STEP 3.

"FARMHOUSE IN THE
POCONOS"

*Begin with sky, then come
forward: hills, tree trunks,
foliage, walls and roofs of
buildings. Observe forms
as well as colors and values.*

"Towers of Angkor Wat" one of the world's most mysterious buildings.

"Abandoned Church, Leningrad" a commentary on a changing world.

STEP 2.

STEP 3.

"CROWDS OF HONG KONG"

Lay out main walls and floors of buildings. Paint rooms behind windows, dark or light, and signs. Window frames, Chinese characters, crowds, all details come later.

STEP 2.

STEP 3.

"SITTING NUDE"

Make a good layout. Paint the figure in its actual colors, add floor and background close to the figure, without leaving hard outlines. Go into more details gradually. Do not overwork your figure.

"Pagoda in Bangkok" colorfully inlaid with broken chinaware.

"Giant Tree in Kowloon". Glowing neon signs behind one of the famous trees on Hong Kong's Kowloon Peninsula. The tree is done in impasto.

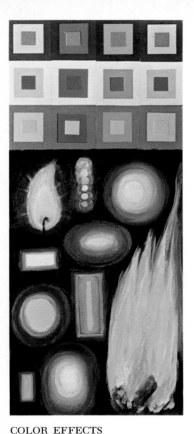

COLOR EFFECTS

Colors play tricks on your eyes. Find out, largely through experimentation, how one color affects another. The same color looks different with every background.

"VILLAGE ON A NILE CANAL"

Reflections in the water are underneath the actual objects, rippled by the water, but quite recognizable. Usually, the reflected image is hazier than the actual scenery.

"STILL LIFE WITH SILVER PITCHER"

Shiny metal reflects just like a mirror. Concave and convex shapes distort all forms, but not colors. Keen observation is necessary in this subject.

"BRIGHT LIGHTS OF BROADWAY"

I tried to capture the gaudiness, brilliance, noise and theatricality of New York's Great White Way in a semi-abstract style. The dark skyscrapers are in strong contrast with the multi-colored illumination of the street.

"MORAINE LAKE NEAR BANFF"

My aim was to render the majestic view of a blue lake among huge rocky mountains. I used impasto in the sky, the water, the rocks and the taller trees.

"BIG CITY"

A collage made of corrugated board, various awnings and other textiles, tarpaper, real rocks and pebbles, glued with polymer and white paste.

7. Landscape Painting

Landscape painting, as we understand it, was introduced by the artists of Holland, in response to the principles of the Reformation. Previously, scenery served only as a backdrop or locale for figure compositions. Although primarily, "landscape" means a picture of the earth as nature has created it, we use the term to include any view of the countryside in which natural scenery plays a vital rôle, even if man-made roads, houses and other objects are parts of the view. The subject is immense, yet the selection of a theme is not as easy as it may sound because what looks magnificent in nature may not be so impressive in a painting. It is not enough to paint a beautiful tree, you must also make it fit into the entire picture.

Make a few pencil sketches and do some telescoping: push an interesting cluster of trees closer to a barn; move a whole mountain, if it will make your composition more attractive. Most artists take a number of photographs and combine the best features of each into one painting. My advice is that you prepare a color sketch on the spot; otherwise, your scenery is likely to look stilted, artificial. Start your landscape from actual observation even if you finish it at home.

FEATURES OF LANDSCAPE PAINTING

Do not paint clouds with hard edges as if they were cut out of paper.

Follow the swirling storm clouds with your brush, in various grays, with the sun breaking through a hole or two in a slightly yellowish tone.

Paint distant mountains just a couple of shades darker than the sky; make colors stronger and add details as the hills approach the foreground.

Watch the endless motion of waves. They are never exactly alike, yet are always similar at the same time and place.

Some rocks are angular, others rounded; their colors differ greatly and may sparkle in the sun.

Do the skeleton of the tree before the foliage. Use small strokes for the leaves, indicating their lace-like delicacy, especially around the edges.

How To Paint a Landscape:

STEP-BY-STEP DEMONSTRATION

"Farmhouse in the Poconos," shown in color on page 47, is based on a color sketch carefully executed on the spot. When I turned it into a full-fledged work, however, I made several changes, such as elongating the wooden structures and pushing the two trees on the right closer to the farm than they really were. I also altered the direction of the dirt road leading to the barn-garage considerably, in order to make it an integral part of the picture. In reality, the road, hardly noticeable from the weeds, leads to the left, out of the picture.

Step 1. The adjacent illustration shows the final layout for my landscape, on a somewhat long board. It is a good outline drawing, omitting small details, such as branches of trees, planks in the buildings or window frames. I went over the charcoal with a thin yellow ochre outline and wiped the charcoal off. Smudges do not affect the paint, charcoal particles do.

To follow the progress of the painting, refer to the color illustrations on page 47.

Final drawing for "Farmhouse in the Poconos"

Step 2. In painting a landscape, you begin with the background, not with the objects as with still life. It would be absurd to paint houses, trees, foliage first, then to try painting sky and clouds around such details.

Start by painting the sky straight across the entire top part of the board, but do not apply the paint so thickly that you blot out the outlines of tree branches and foliage. Instead of painting exactly to the outlines of roofs and hills, cross into those parts with the sky. Paint the clouds, too. Polymer dries fast and you can now paint the distant hills, in very light tones of blue-violet, just a couple of shades darker than the sky in order to keep the hills far in the distance so that the trees and structures will stand out clearly.

Paint tree branches, in grayish-brown, not black, behind roofs and in the distance. Indicate the various colors in the walls of buildings (gray, ochre, burnt sienna, red, orange), the main shadows on the right sidewall of each building section; the darkness within the garage, and paint a few strokes in the roofs, the road, the weedy ground. Work all over the board, a little here, a little there, with enough water to make the paint flow smoothly over the rough surface without flooding.

Now work on the foliage behind the roofs and in the distance, just this side of the hills, going behind the buildings in order to avoid leaving white spots or outlines. Remember that trees are not huge sheets of green wool thrown over wooden hatracks. They consist of trunk, main and smaller branches, the skeleton of a tree, so to speak, and leaves growing out of the branches. We need not paint every single leaf, but we must at least indicate that there are leaves. Do them in short strokes, with the tip of a round or small flat brush, observing the shape, size, and color of each large section of foliage, especially dark and light sections. Green is not the same green all over. There are many nuances, from bright yellow-green to purplish-green, blue-green, and so forth.

The foreground has brownish-violet patches of earth and orange-green dried-out grass and weed. Do the earth with horizontal strokes, the weed with upright ones. Paint tree trunks in the middleground before adding their foliage. For the near trees, use brighter greens, darker shadows, to differentiate these from the ones farther away.

Step 3. You do not need photographic details to achieve realism unless you wish to be a "magic realist." Add details as you go on working, but never minute ones. Your painting is much smaller than reality; paint only as much as you can actually see. There are the dilapidated planks of the old structures; perhaps not one of them is straight; many of them have some old paint left, others are weatherbeaten. You can see window frames ready to fall off their rusty hinges, but you cannot see small cracks from a distance. Colors are more important, esthetically more satisfying, than tiny knots in the wood, painted on so small a scale.

Step 4. The finished painting has the colors and textures of planks, weed, road, the stakes of the fences, cast shadows on the ground, and the structures.

The barn-garage has enough depth, and you can distinguish the old car in it without seeing the numbers on the registration plate. I applied thicker paint in a few spots for textural variety and interest. The picture shows a clear day when all colors are sparkling but does not exaggerate them. This is not a glamorized farm, but a picturesque one. It is part of the scenery. No section is more important than the others; the effect is one of unity. It is normally better to stop when this result is achieved than go on and perhaps overwork your painting.

OTHER LANDSCAPE SUBJECTS

Connecticut River Valley scene. The day was overcast and gray.

Wooden house in Pennsylvania. Shabby structures are often more interesting to paint than great mansions.

Oaxaca, Mexico, seen from a hilltop. Rich coloring round the town enhances the whiteness of the adobe houses.

Small villas among interesting trees in Sydney, Australia.

8. Seascape Painting

During the past hundred years or so, the sea has become a popular subject for painting. The ever-changing colors and moods of the sea, the variety of shorelines, the graceful and formidable motions of the waves are a great source of inspiration. Ships and boats add to the wealth of this subject. To portray the sea, much observation is necessary. Study rocks, waves, beaches, shacks, boats. The painting procedure is the same as in landscape: start with the sky, the background, coming forward gradually, with brighter, more contrasty hues. The sea itself is horizontal, but the shores slant according to the angle from which you view them.

The higher you go the more water you see; the lower your eye level, the higher the shoreline. My advice is, once again: make sketches in pencil and in color before commencing to work on a large painting.

Seascape is a highly specialized subject. The ramifications of the various moods of the water, the different kinds of waves and surf, the characteristics of boats and ships of all sorts, from dinghies through clipper ships, frigates, fishing trawlers, catamarans to our modern luxury liners, are so great that much research is necessary. Neither waves nor sailing ships, neither seagulls nor motorboats can be painted without a practical knowledge of all these ingredients of seascapes. I suggest for a start that you paint the sea as part of a landscape with a view of the sea.

SOME SEASCAPE SUBJECTS

Seascape viewed from a mountain in Sicily

Lighthouse in New England, seen from a low shore.

Waterfront in Manila. Reflections in the water are directly under the objects, in perspective.

9. Reflections

REFLECTIONS IN WATER

Water in a large mass, sea, lake, or river, is a shiny substance. Smooth water is like a mirror, except that a mirror may be placed in any position whereas water is always horizontal. Only objects on the shore and above the water are reflected in it. You can see yourself if you bend over a mirror-smooth lake or pool; your right hand appears to be the left and vice versa, just as in a true mirror. Reflections in water are inverted images. The top of a tree or the roof of a house is at the bottom of the painting, but every part of the reflected image is directly underneath the actual object, seen in the same perspective as the actual view.

Except for occasional moments of absolute stillness, water ripples, so that the edges of reflected images are slightly broken up in constant motion. There are differences in tones; even the brightest colors are slightly bluish or greenish in reflections. The best way to paint reflections in water is to do them simultaneously with the actual scenery. In my "Village on a Nile Canal" (see color illustration on page 54), I painted typical Egyptian adobe houses above the shoreline in main masses and immediately painted their reflections in the same hues: gray, green, blue, pink, and so forth. As I painted the balconies almost all Egyptian village houses have, I also indicated them in the water in the same proportion below the shore as they were above in the actual structures. Doors, windows, the poles supporting the balconies were all painted directly underneath the real ones, but in a rippled manner. I also quickly brushed the colors in the water into each other and rippled them around the edges. The fast-drying polymer enabled me to go over the water with transparent washes of greenish ochre to suggest the dirty water in the canal. A few broken lines in white and pale blue show the motion of the water and the reflection of the clear blue sky.

I had sketches of Egyptian men in long cloaks talking to each other near the edge of the water and women dressed in black walking with big baskets on their heads. I placed these in the picture without small details and added their reflections.

REFLECTIONS IN METAL AND GLASS

Highly polished metal reflects like a mirror. As a matter of fact, ancient civilizations used metal mirrors in the shape of our own feminine hand mirrors. Reflections in metal behave in the same fashion as in a regular mirror. The slightest flaw distorts the reflection. Everybody knows the trick-mirrors in amusement parks; one mirror makes you seem emaciated, tall; another one turns you into a terribly fat and short person; still another distorts you into a nightmarish monster. On a smaller scale, distortions occur on any curved, polished surface, such as a rounded silver bowl or any round glass with a dark background.

Reflections on a curved surface must be observed with care and drawn from a single viewpoint. If you move, the reflected image moves with you and becomes distorted in a different way. Rounded metal and glass, especially of a concave shape, also diminish the image like a lens.

Polished metal reflects its surroundings. You can render metal or glass by observing all reflections in it. Do not try to paint a silver bowl in silver paint. Look at the appearance of the object; paint what you see, and the result will look like silver or glass.

"Still Life with Silver Pitcher" (see color illustration on page 54), was planned to show reflections in a bright silver pitcher, the lower part of which is convex while its neck is concave, and in a not-so-highly polished rectangular tin box. Two apples, one yellow, the other red, on white and pink paper napkins are reflected in these metal objects. Even the flat metal reduces the sizes; in the convex part of the pitcher, the apples are considerably thinner and smaller, the paper napkins follow the shape of the pitcher. In the neck of the silver pitcher, the apples are no bigger than a couple of cherries but can still be recognized.

The reflections of three large windows of my studio can be clearly seen on the neck of the pitcher. The objects were arranged on a waxed table in which vague reflections of the colors of the apples and the highlights of the metal box can be seen. It took serious observation to execute this painting, but it was an exciting kind of work and the result is an attractive traditional still life.

10. Cityscape Painting

A city, with its buildings, streets, crowds and traffic, can be just as picturesque as natural scenery. Even such commercial places as New York's Wall Street, London's Piccadilly Circus, and the Champs Elysées of Paris have inspired many an artist. There is beauty in the variety of edifices; the endless, colorful traffic of cars, buses, throngs; store signs; the mood of the place; the time of the day; the weather. Towards evening, lights begin to appear which, on a hazy day, imbue the city with mellowness. A night scene with its thousands of lamps and signs takes your breath away.

The Far East, the Near East and North Africa have exotic towns. Narrow, winding streets, shabby walls, ancient ruins and colorful laundry on balconies make Mediterranean cities eternally stimulating to the artist. The towering skyscrapers of the New World have their own magic. We also have slums and even though we regret their existence, we find them good subjects for painting.

In the Old World, people are accustomed to artists painting in the streets. In America, passers-by, especially kids, drive you away or drive you crazy, but you can draw a quick sketch or two and snap a couple of photographs before this happens. Lay the painting out, return to the spot for additional sketches and notes, if possible.

How To Paint a Cityscape:

STEP-BY-STEP DEMONSTRATION

One of the most exciting cities to paint is the British Crown Colony of Hong Kong, which includes the Kowloon Peninsula. It is a city now fantastically overcrowded, with houses somewhat whimsically enlarged to accommodate the influx of people, thousands of signs, almost always in Chinese, an incredible variety of colors. What makes Hong Kong houses so picturesque is that new floors have been built atop old buildings, each new floor the same size as the old one, of course, but in an amazingly or amusingly different style. Even the most modern buildings exude an Oriental atmosphere.

My painting "Crowds of Hong Kong" (see color illustration on page 50), created on the basis of many sketches and pictures, is not a factual representation, but anyone who has ever been in that city will recognize it. I never paint exact replicas of what I see, but combine elements I consider interesting and/or attractive and try to be faithful to the spirit of the place.

Even though distortions are permissible, a knowledge of perspective in a cityscape is almost mandatory, unless you want to represent a city devastated by an earthquake. Study the chapter on perspective, page 25, and employ receding lines. Observe color perspective by painting distant parts in lighter tones. Watch especially the vertical lines. The surest way of drawing them is by measuring the distance along a few of these lines from the left or right edge of the board.

Step 1. The final outline drawing for my painting "Crowds of Hong Kong," in thin yellow ochre, is the result of several sketches, some in horizontal, others in an upright shape. My outlines refer only to the basic construction and proportions of walls, floors, windows, the largest store signs, omitting detail. I allow the houses on the right to run off the top of the board in order to suggest greater height; I cut the bottoms off since I want room to show the wavelike motion and density of a typical crowd in Hong Kong. The crowd is not outlined or even indicated here; it will be painted after the rest is finished. Perspective is not forgotten, but nothing in this layout is unalterable. It is merely a guide to my painting; I must have the main sizes of houses and floors, with a good distribution of forms in windows and walls.

To follow the development of the painting, refer to the color reproductions on page 50.

Vertical lines often come out on a slant, giving the impression that the buildings are about to collapse.

void this by measuring the distance of a few ain uprights from the left or right edge of the oard.

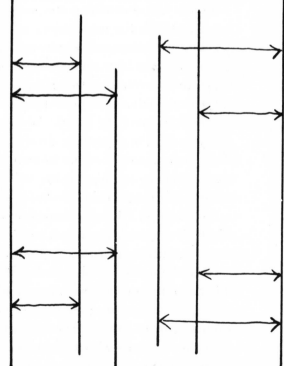

Final layout for "Crowds of Hong Kong"

Step 2. Using enough water to spread the paint quickly but without dripping, I establish the main colors with a three-quarter-inch flat bristle brush. Many of the casement windows cover the entire front of a room. Through the small panes, you see curtains, lights or darkness, but at first, I am only interested in recording the dark purplish spaces behind the windows, without worrying about the grilled patterns of the window frames.

I work all over the board. Add more colors to walls, floors; delineate as well as paint the signs more carefully; suggest curtains or light in some windows; paint a couple of bright awnings and the reflections of the sky in certain windowpanes. I paint the yellowish, greenish lights or the blue-white reflections where they are to be, before doing any of the window frames.

Step 3. Now I develop more detail, using less diluted paint. Some parts of the walls are thickly painted. I also begin to paint the window frames with their multiplicity of patterns. The store window comes next with the lower parts of the walls. I apply a few dashes suggesting the crowd. The people in this painting are faceless, moving like waves, in Western or Eastern garments. Many men are in white shirtsleeves; some women wear gaily colored Chinese gowns. I make strokes of various colors, one here, one there, not in a regular, mechanical pattern, to indicate the way people are dressed, some in blue, others in brown, gray, red, pink, and so forth. Gradually, I add suggestions of skirts, trousers, perhaps a large pocketbook or suitcase in a hand, keeping them unobtrusive. Spots serve for the heads: light ones for faces, dark ones for those I see from the rear. Some men are carrying big trays over the heads of the throng, a common sight in Hong Kong. A few jinrikishas may be seen with their convertible tops and large wheels.

Step 4. The big signs are all in Chinese, occasionally with English words underneath in very small letters. I want to suggest the intricate and artistic Chinese characters without rendering them exactly. Many Chinese characters resemble each other very closely, with no more difference between them than let us say between the O and the Q or the E and the F of our Latin alphabet. The slightest error on my part in copying the Chinese characters might make them meaningless or, what is worse, might give them an entirely different, perhaps most unpleasant, meaning. I follow the same procedure when I paint a cityscape with signs in the Latin alphabet and do not wish to advertise a certain name or product by painting Latin letters without assembling them in a legible manner.

To finish off, I add more strokes to the crowd; go over certain parts of houses and signs with a variety of washes, toning one section down, making another part dirtier looking.

PAINTING CROWDS AND STREET TRAFFIC

The technique of painting a street crowd is illustrated in Step 3 of the foregoing demonstration. Occasionally, however, you may wish to paint a smaller group, with two or three prominent figures in the foreground. You might show them from the waist or the knees up, with a more accurate definition of the clothing, shirts, neckties, jackets, hats, though still without tiny details. Paint the figures in the background with a few strokes. Detailed little figures, of the kind done by Henri Rousseau and Grandma Moses, have their charm, but belong to the primitive school. If you paint such figures your whole work must be done in the same naive manner.

Vehicular traffic depends upon the city and time of day. Make sketches and photographs of cars, buses, from the front, rear, and side, according to the angle from which you are painting the scene. Vehicles in the distance appear smaller and hazier. Note the styles of automobiles: they change frequently in America, while many antiquated models are still to be seen in Old World cities. Remember that traffic proceeds on the left in a large part of the world. Don't paint cars driving on the right-hand side of the street in cityscapes of Britain, Sweden and most of the Far East! But don't get bogged down in details. Too many may detract from the effect of motion that really counts in a street scene.

Even when you paint distinct figures in the foreground of a crowd, avoid minute details.

When painting crowds, a few strokes in whatever colors may be typical of the place and the season can suggest the upper bodies of people.

Add more random strokes, in diverse hues, in lower section, to indicate skirts, trousers.

Dark spots serve for heads seen from back, light ones for faces. A few more touches add legs, arms, perhaps a large pocketbook or package.

Cars, buses should be presented in the sketchiest manner. You are painting traffic in motion, not an ad for a new car.

Facing traffic. Observe whether it is right-handed or left-handed traffic.

OTHER CITYSCAPE SUBJECTS

*In a Sicilian town, each house is different, and
often shabby.*

*The Casbah, notorious inner city of Algiers, pic-
turesque, and not really dangerous.*

*Town in Tunisia, with colorful crowds and awn-
ings against whitewashed buildings.*

CITIES AT NIGHT

Whether you are in New York or Tokyo, Berlin or Rio de Janeiro, Baghdad or Casablanca, night turns big cities into wonderlands. The dazzling illumination, moving signs, neon lights, and bright store windows disguise the shabbiness plainly and painfully visible by daylight. It is exciting to paint such a scene. In my painting "Bright Lights of Broadway" (see page 54), I laid the pattern out in large masses on a tall, narrow board, mostly in dark hues, but differentiating between the greenish blue sky and buildings of diverse tones, such as cobalt violet mixed with black, phthalocyanine green mixed with cadmium red, burnt sienna combined with ultramarine blue. I used lighter tones for the lower sections of houses, avoiding, however, positive outlines for buildings and stores. I wanted this painting to give an idea of the superficial splendor of New York's "Great White Way," its innumerable signs, both around the stores and theater entrances and high above the sidewalks, atop small houses as well as skyscrapers.

I painted lights shining through some windows, reflections in other windowpanes, the illuminated signs in all the colors of the rainbow. I applied many of the lights in impasto so that they sparkle as the outside light hits them. I merely suggested crowds and the tops of cars and buses at the bottom of the picture. The illuminated windows in the houses are not nearly as bright as the lighted signs and stores. A feeling of depth exists even at night. I painted many colors on top of each other before I was satisfied with the effect, which may now be called either semi-abstract or semi-realistic. I wanted to capture the atmosphere of the spectacular scene, rather than a photographic resemblance.

11. Figure Painting

The ancient Greeks were the first to show the human face and figure in a realistic, if idealized, manner, emphasizing graceful proportions and physical beauty of the body either in the nude or in form-accentuating drapery. Admiration for the nude came back with the Renaissance when most paintings and sculpture were devoted to the human figure. Although today the general public neither understands nor buys paintings featuring the naked human body, our art schools recognize the importance of depicting the nude figure in developing skill and artistry in general.

Professional models are normally required for working from life, so it is mostly done in art schools or art groups. Before starting to work from life, I recommend that you draw from plaster casts because these are easier to study and to measure than live models who cannot remain absolutely still. Then do some quick sketching of figures in action which teaches you how to observe and jot down positions assumed in walking, standing, sitting, reclining. Drawing from life is a difficult project, but well worth trying. Once you know how to draw and paint a human figure, other subjects will seem much easier.

How To Paint a Nude Figure:

STEP-BY-STEP DEMONSTRATION

First, find a professional model, rather than trying to paint a friend or relative. A model can retain the same position for twenty-five minutes or so, and can resume it after every period of rest, day after day. You have to mark the main points of the figure. Make an outline for feet, hands, knees, buttocks or whichever part of the model touches chair, table or platform. The marking is best done with Scotch masking tape which can be removed when the painting is finished, but will not rub off like chalk marks would.

Second, select a pose. Allow the model to find a natural position. Contorted, unusual positions may be sketched quickly or photographed, but are unsuitable for long poses. It is distracting when your model has to stretch out kinks every few minutes.

Avoid complete profiles, which are usually "flat" in appearance and difficult to turn into interesting paintings. Avoid a standing position in which the nude faces you squarely and resembles a manikin in a store window before being dressed. Do not use immense amounts of drapery on the chair or behind the model. Finally, keep the pose in good taste.

Stand or sit far enough from the model to hold the entire figure within your circle of vision. In other words, you have to see the model's head and feet without looking up or down.

Make sure to have a board or canvas to suit the pose. You can hardly paint a tall, standing model on a horizontal board or a long, reclining figure on a square or an upright board, unless other elements of the composition require it. Consider the whole composition, not merely the figure, before you start. Unfortunately, many teachers and students consider it a virtue, a symbol of great knowledge and talent, to begin a work directly with brush and paint. The result, more often than not, is poor composition, a misplaced figure floating in mid-air, too small or too big, with top of head, toes, fingers, a knee or an elbow cruelly chopped off, not for esthetic reasons, not as a matter of artistic freedom, but through sheer accident. I recommend that you do a charcoal sketch first, preferably on a sheet of tracing paper covering your board. Once you have a satisfactory sketch, go over the charcoal in pencil, wipe the charcoal off, and trace the drawing on your board. The tracing paper can easily be shifted up or down, right or left, in order to find the correct place for the figure in the final layout. This extra work of fifteen to twenty minutes is likely to save you not only much correcting and changing, it may very well save your entire painting.

anding nude ought to be painted on tall, narrow board. Drapery cannot artistically fill the big mpty space.

Side view of sitting model is uninteresting.

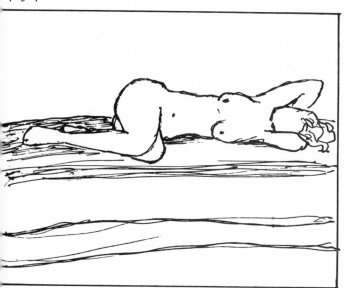

Reclining nude should be done on long horizontal board instead of a standard-shaped one on which it seems to be floating upwards.

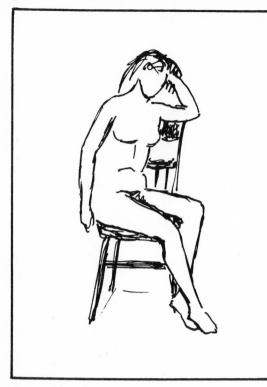

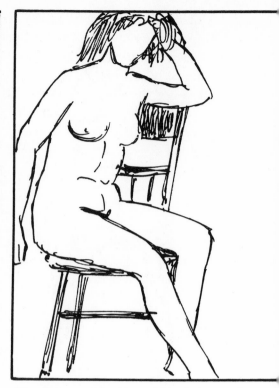

Figure is much too small and too high up.

Figure is too big. Top of head, feet and part of right arm are cut out of the picture.

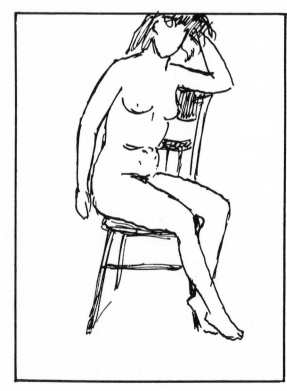

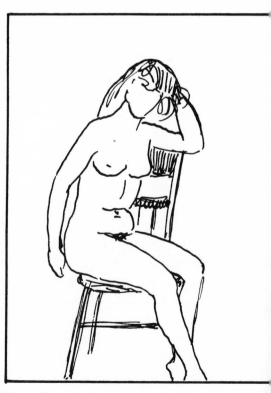

Top of head cut off, although there is ample space on the board.

Toes chopped off, with plenty of room above the head.

Final layout for "Sitting Nude"

The woman who posed for the painting "Sitting Nude," shown in color on page 51, was Claude, one of Matisse's last and finest models.

I made the charcoal drawing on tracing paper. The four illustrations above show how easy it would have been to lay the work out in a silly fashion, cutting one part or another of the figure off by accident. The most common mistake made by art students is to start a figure too high and exactly in the center of the picture.

Step 1. The final drawing for my painting is shown on this page. As always, I went over the charcoal outlines with a thin yellow ochre, wiping the charcoal off before applying paint.

Refer to the color illustrations of this work's development on page 51.

Step 2. Paint lightest and darkest parts first. Be not afraid of shadows; make them strong. Work in short strokes, in different directions, rather than trying to follow the forms with the brush. It is all right to do that in pen-and-ink drawings, but a thigh is not going to look rounded if you paint it with curved brush strokes. It wll look as if it were a Mexican straw figure. Shading creates a feeling of roundness. Do not fall into the common error of painting the entire figure in what is popularly called "fleshcolor"; paint each part the way it looks: ochre, pink, slightly violet tones, with shadows ranging from greenish brown to bluish purple. Observe colors and values. Do not mix any color with black in this painting because black gives a dirty-looking tone. Only the hair may be actually black in any nude.

Work only on the main forms. Paint floor and background next to the figure, working away from or toward the figure, leaving it soft rather than outlining it like a paper doll. Indicate the chair not only as part of the picture, but because it helps you in determining the positions of elbow, hand, thigh, knees, feet.

Step 3. Continue brushwork, correcting colors and values, blending colors into each other where necessary. Step back, every now and then; try to judge the general effect of lights and shadows. It is a good idea to turn your back on the painting, holding a small mirror in such a manner that you can see both the model and your work simultaneously. This enables you to compare the two.

Do not treat the head as if it were a portrait. Indicate eyes, tip of nose, mouth, shadows, lights. Paint the skin under the hair, then do the hair with a somewhat worn bristle brush, rather dry, pulling it into the face and also over the background in order to give it the texture it really has.

Step 4. Finishing depends upon you, as always. Do you intend to paint a pin-up girl? Or do you want to study human forms and colors? It requires a great deal of skill to turn out a pin-up girl, but that is commercial art. As a general principle, it is best to paint only as much as you really see from a distance. Leave your work sketchy rather than overwork it.

BACKGROUND FOR NUDES

A very light background makes the figure look like a commercial design, a calendar picture; a very dark one, often done by art students, makes the painting too flashy. It is easy to make the figure stand out against a dark backdrop, but subtlety is preferable to such commonplace effects.

Students often try to paint the entire room, usually a studio in a school, just as it happens to be, including stools, easels, perhaps a screen behind which the model keeps her or his garments. Such a background demands a great deal of thinking, experimenting and knowledge. It must also be done in sufficiently subdued tones to keep it behind the model. Still other students devise an imaginary setting, such as the model sitting on a park bench or reclining in the grass. This kind of background may be fun and it turns a study of a nude into a kind of pretty picture. The best idea is the simplest as well as the most professional. It is to paint the background in a color which suits the figure, and to paint it in a variety of tones, rather than in one flat color.

COSTUME PAINTING

Artists use the term "costume" in reference to clothes of any kind worn by their models. Most contemporary figure painting is of the costumed variety. An experienced artist first draws the general proportions and foreshortening

Coat on chair drapes according to the shape of the chair.

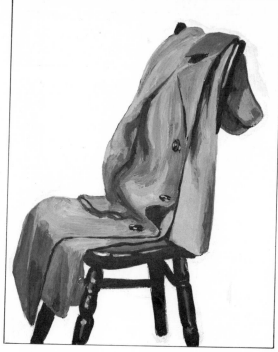

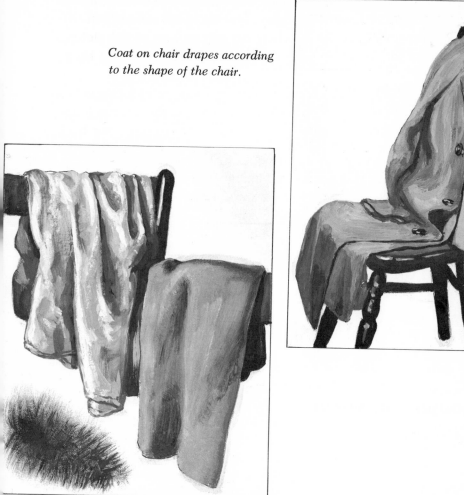

Upper left: *silk dress, shiny, with crisp folds.* On right: *woolen skirt, few folds, no strong highlights.* Lower left: *a piece of fur, done with a dry brush, pulled from center toward the fine ends, in slightly different directions.*

of the naked figure, before he paints the apparel. Clothing folds, hangs, and drapes according to what is inside of or underneath it.

In this project, as in all others, concentrate on sizes, shapes, colors, lights and shadows; forget about details. Texture is of great significance. You can recognize certain materials, such as silk, velvet, wool, from a distance. Paint such materials in a realistic manner. Silk is crisp and shiny; wool is dull, with soft folds. If you paint the highlights and shadows on a woolen skirt in sharp contrast, the result will look like silk.

Study clothes by painting an overcoat or jacket thrown on the back of a chair; see how it folds and drapes, how the buttons are different from every angle. Put a silk blouse on a hanger and observe its many folds, its sharp highlights. Hats, gloves, pocketbooks, scarves make good still life subjects, even if you are not interested in painting costumed figures.

12. Other Uses for Polymer

Stage Backdrops and Props: Polymer is absolutely ideal for painting stage curtains, backdrops and props. It dries fast and waterproof, and remains flexible indefinitely. You need not worry about rain. The scenery may be rolled up and transported or stored. Such theatrical work used to be done with cheap pigments mixed with hot, foul-smelling fish or rabbit glue. The colors were dull, the material creased and cracked easily; water damaged it irreparably. Polymer gives perfect results, without any odor. Props constructed of cheap materials not only look good when painted in polymer, but the plastic color, especially when used with glossy varnish, protects them.

Furniture Decoration: Inexpensive unfinished furniture can be turned into charming and permanent pieces with the help of polymer. You can let your imagination run riot. Use gesso or extender; decorations may be in any color, thin or thick. If you use impasto, you might scratch designs into it. Holes, cracks are easy to cover, just add more paint. Matte or glossy varnish gives your furniture extra protection.

Luggage: If you travel, you know what a chore it often is to find your luggage in a pile. After all, every suitcase is manufactured by the thousands. Decorate yours in polymer and you will have no problem in picking it out. Polymer works on plastic and metal luggage directly. On leather, you have to wash the part you intend to decorate with a little denatured alcohol. Highly polished leather goods, however, may not take polymer.

You need not paint fancy pictures on your valise. A stripe, a spot, your initials or any distinguishing mark in color that stands out, on each side of your luggage, will enable you to identify it quickly.

Textiles: Any textile may be decorated with polymer, either directly or over a thin coat of gesso applied to the material. Polymer does not interfere with the flexibility of the textile; it will not crack or peel; washing will not harm it.

Toys: Thick paint or extender can create novel effects on old toys. You can also repair toys by gluing broken parts together; merely use lots of paint and hold the broken sections together for a couple of minutes. The colors are non-toxic. Add glossy medium or varnish the toy with it and you have a practically scuffproof object.

Frames: Turn the cheapest molding into an elegant frame by creating designs with the extender. This is also perfect for repairing old ornamental frames. Apply the extender gradually, in layers, and paint the frame when it is dry. If you make your own frames, you are likely to have difficulties with the mitering. A little ornament in each corner, made with extender and polymer, will beautifully camouflage your mistakes.

Lampshades: Since polymer works on all the plastics from which lampshades are made, and since it can be applied in transparent washes as well as in opaque blobs, it is excellent for decorating lampshades. Test various colors, thicknesses of paint, and diverse brush strokes, before doing the actual work.

Every polymer color can be made transparent by adding water or gel to it, but varying thicknesses of paint result in different degrees of transparency. Crude, uneven brush strokes are not attractive when light shines through them. Practice against a lighted bulb, either by working on a piece of material attached to a lampshade or by placing the material on a glasstop table illuminated from below.

Interesting stained-glass window effects can be achieved by dripping thick outlines on the material, in a floral or abstract design, then painting the spaces between outlines in transparent glazes. Do the outlines on the outside, the transparent coloring on the inside of the lampshade, so that the brilliant colors will only be seen when the light is on, but the decorative design on the outside is always visible.

Fences: Polymer is easier to apply to a fence than cheap household oil paint and offers a much bigger selection of hues. Add glossy medium or varnish the fence with it in order to obtain absolute protection against the vicissitudes of weather.

You will find other uses for polymer. If the surface you want to paint is too smooth, scratch it with sandpaper or a wire brush so the paint adheres better. In outdoor work, pure colors are recommended. For example, use ready-made orange instead of mixing red and yellow. Fine differences of shades are normally not required in outdoor decorations. The use of unmixed colors on large surfaces is always more practical than trying to mix a big batch of color, especially when so many ready-made ones are available.

13. Oil-Mixed Polymer

Certain plastic colors are made to be thinned with turpentine or any other oil painting medium. These adhere to any surface, including oily canvas, and dry in a few hours. The drying time may be retarded by adding more turpentine or a special medium for oil-plastics, but the moment you add turpentine you lose one of the most valuable characteristics of polymer: the fact that it does not yellow with age. Employed without such ingredients, oil plastics do not discolor, but it is practically impossible to work with them without thinning them with at least a small amount of turpentine.

Oil-plastics dry fast on the surface but remain soft underneath, and if you apply several layers, one on top of the other, you have to isolate each with a plastic oil varnish which dries in a few minutes and allows you to build your paint up as you wish. The same varnish serves as a final protective varnish, and may also be applied over regular oil paintings.

In the final analysis, oil-plastics have only one advantage over regular oil colors: they dry faster. Their single advantage over plastic watercolors lies in the fact that they adhere to oily surfaces, too. On the other hand, the immense advantage of watercolor polymer over oil polymer is that it is mixed with water and does not discolor in any manner; hands, brushes are washed in water which is available anywhere.

Furthermore, many persons are allergic to turpentine and the odor of oil colors. Water polymer has no odor and nobody has been known to be allergic to it. Ultimately, oil polymers cannot take the place of regular oil colors, whereas water polymers are an entirely new concept in painting, offering infinite and remarkable possibilities.

14. Tips to Painters

SIZES AND SHAPES

The size and shape of your painting depend upon your subject as well as your temperament. You may like to work on a large scale; you may prefer small paintings. You are unlikely to paint a seascape on a tall, narrow, upright panel and just as unlikely to feature sequoias on a very low, very wide horizontal board. Whatever shapes and sizes you prefer, try not to have too many different ones and consider the advisability of using certain standard sizes, such as 18x24 inches, 20x30 inches, 22x28 inches, 22x30 inches, 30x40 inches, which come out of full sheets or boards with little, if any, waste. For larger paintings, canvas may be necessary. Masonite and other boards used in building are available in large sizes but should be nailed to strips in order to protect the corners and edges.

You can buy ready-made frames for standard sized paintings at reasonable prices. If you must have odd sizes, figure out what you can get from a full sheet or board without waste. For instance, a 40x60-inch board may be cut into four 20x30, two 20x60, or two 30x40-inch pieces. Although a 3:4 ratio in shapes is pleasing to the eye, tall, narrow, or long, horizontal formats have also become popular. The chances are you will need several different shapes and sizes but, for practical and economic reasons, stick to a few, and have a couple of frames for each. This will enable you to change pictures without the necessity of ordering a new frame each time you have to exhibit a painting. You can thus solve a problem of expense and storage as well.

VARNISHING

Polymer paintings may be varnished as soon as they are finished, not a year-and-a-half or two later, as with oils. Plastic varnish is the same as the medium and comes in matte and glossy versions. Both are white and thick, and when you first use this varnish you are bound to get a shock. You believe the painting is ruined because the varnish looks like buttermilk.

Always add water to the varnish, either by mixing it in a clean cup or by constantly dipping your brush in water while varnishing the painting. Make sure to use enough water and apply the varnish evenly, with a wide brush, first in one direction, then the other, keeping it wet all the time. When finished, run a clean, squeezed-out brush along the four edges of the board to pick up the excess varnish.

All varnishing ought to be done flat on a table in a dust-free room. Wait ten to fifteen minutes before standing the painting up. The thick, white varnish soon becomes crystal-clear. The glossy varnish is considerably shinier than the matte varnish. I recommend the matte varnish for paintings to hang on walls, the glossy varnish for outdoor purposes.

On very rough boards, add more water to the varnish than on a smooth one and try to keep it from collecting in the crevices because, occasionally, white spots appear in such a case. If this "snow" effect does not develop within a half hour or so, it will not occur at all. Should it happen, go over the entire surface immediately with a clean, wet brush, rub the varnish a little and distribute it more evenly. Varnish is full protection for polymer paintings. Using glass in the framing is not necessary.

FRAMING

Frames do not make paintings, but they can work for them or against them. The best frame cannot transform a bad picture into a masterpiece, but a masterpiece can be damaged, esthetically, by a bad frme. Most art exhibitions require simple but proper framing. "Proper" means that the frame should have the right width, depth and strength for the painting it surrounds. Avoid very ornate frames for exhibiting purposes. Buy an unfinished frame and finish it yourself, with gesso or extender. The colors of the frame should harmonize with those of the picture. If your painting has much warm coloring, such as red, orange, brown, give your frame tints of these hues. The coloring can quickly be changed if a different painting demands it.

EXHIBITING

It is nice to paint for the sake of painting, but whether you admit it or not, your true goal is to exhibit your work. There are countless local art associations, clubs, cultural groups with annual or seasonal exhibitions. Many are open to amateurs as well as professionals, offering awards to the best entries in separate categories. Join such groups if possible, because participation is stimulating and you have an opportunity to compare your work with that of others. Ultimately you may hope to "hang" in a national exhibition, where your entry has to pass a jury of selection.

Art magazines have Exhibition Opportunities columns listing regional and national exhibitions. Send a postcard to any of these shows (the address is in the listing) asking the secretary to place you on the mailing list. You will automatically receive notices of forthcoming exhibitions. Never enter your work without first obtaining the official prospectus and entry forms. Read the prospectus carefully; observe size, medium, shipping instructions, receiving and removal dates, fees. Polymer, like casein, is regarded as one of the aquamedia if it is framed like a watercolor, in a mat, under glass. If it is framed like an oil painting, it goes before the oil jury of selection. As polymer grows in popularity, it will have a section of its own in major exhibitions.

The prospectus usually gives a clue to the preference of an art society or of the judges. If you work in the traditional manner, you can hardly expect to have your entry pass the jury of, let us say, the Nonobjective Artists of America; if you do nonobjective work, it is unlikely to be accepted by the Society of Traditional Artists. Many art societies have mixed juries; read the names of the judges and you can tell, after a while, whether they are inclined to favor the style in which you work. However, there is no safe bet in art, just as there is none at the racetrack.

Do not feel heartbroken if your work is rejected. It has happened to the foremost artists; a painting rejected by one jury may win an award in the next show. Whether your work is accepted or not, make a point of seeing the exhibition. Look at the works of other artists. You might get some inspiration in reference to what to paint or what not to paint in the future. Here's wishing you the best possible luck.